ISBN 978-1-331-57022-6
PIBN 10207207

Forgotten Books is a registered trademark of FB &c Ltd.
Copyright © 2018 FB &c Ltd.
FB &c Ltd, Dalton House, 60 Windsor Avenue, London, SW19 2RR.
Company number 08720141. Registered in England and Wales.

For support please visit www.forgottenbooks.com

1 MONTH OF
FREE
READING

at

www.ForgottenBooks.com

By purchasing this book you are eligible for one month membership to ForgottenBooks.com, giving you unlimited access to our entire collection of over 1,000,000 titles via our web site and mobile apps.

To claim your free month visit:

www.forgottenbooks.com/free207207

English
Français
Deutsche
Italiano
Español
Português

www.forgottenbooks.com

Mythology Photography **Fiction**
Fishing Christianity **Art** Cooking
Essays Buddhism Freemasonry
Medicine **Biology** Music **Ancient
Egypt** Evolution Carpentry Physics
Dance Geology **Mathematics** Fitness
Shakespeare **Folklore** Yoga Marketing
Confidence Immortality Biographies
Poetry **Psychology** Witchcraft
Electronics Chemistry History **Law**
Accounting **Philosophy** Anthropology
Alchemy Drama Quantum Mechanics
Atheism Sexual Health **Ancient History**
Entrepreneurship Languages Sport
Paleontology Needlework Islam
Metaphysics Investment Archaeology
Parenting Statistics Criminology
Motivational

The
Stars and
Bars

MAJOR ORREN R. SMITH

Veteran of three wars—in Mexico, in Utah, and the War Between the States.
Designer of the first Confederate Flag.

HISTORY

OF THE

STARS AND BARS

Designed by

ORREN RANDOLPH SMITH

February, 1861

At Louisburg, North Carolina

Adopted by

Congress of Confederate States of America

at Montgomery, Alabama

March 4, 1861

EDWARDS & BROUGHTON PRINTING COMPANY
RALEIGH, NORTH CAROLINA
1913

In Memoriam

The Birth of the Stars and Bars

Be it said to the honor of both herein mentioned, the Veteran of
the Gray, Orren Randolph Smith, designer of the first Confederate
Flag, who died recently at his home in Henderson, North Carolina,
and the Veteran of the Blue, General Edward Albert Lever, who
fought against that flag, and who is the editor of the magazine in
which this poem appears, whatever the convictions of the two men
may have been, each knew the other for a generous foe. Significant of the fact is the silent tribute of regard which *Latin America*
pays to the memory of a gallant soldier gone to his reward.

L. E. Y.

The shadow of a storm brooded o'er all,
    The hearts of men were thrilled with sounds afar,
"What is this gloom that blackens like a pall?
    If war must be," one cried, "then give us war!
Yet I have loved my country; I have cheered
    The Stars and Stripes beneath the Mexic skies;
The bullet of the foe I have not feared!
    All men are brothers—must we break such ties?"

War was declared. Fate rang Hope's funeral knell
    The storm-cloud broke, and the Red, White and Blue—
Flag he had bled for—he must bid farewell;
    He ne'er had thought to recognize a new!
Inexorable decree! Southland so fair,
    From henceforth he was thine and thine alone—
Thine to the uttermost, to do and dare,
    With soul determined, with the last doubt flown!

Home of the free, beloved and peerless land,
    Thou had'st no flag to raise above the fray,
No emblem all thine own to lead thy band,
    The brave, the true, the dauntless men in gray!

"A soldier's flag," he said with kindling glance,
    "Must be his inspiration—something more
Than bunting and gay colors to enhance
    Its meaning and significance." He bore

No bitterness within his lofty soul,
    His great heart had no room for petty hate.
Right was his slogan, Freedom was his goal,
    This Orren Randolph Smith! Whate'er the fate
Of the young Constitution, he would be
    Firt to reveal its emblem to the world!—
Thus musing, he selected symbols three—   ·
    Church, State and Press, on azure field unfurled.

Then seven stars he grouped in circle round—
    One white star for each State—"For I know," he said,
"The Circle hath a meaning most profound,
    Time and Eternity!" Blue, White and Red
He tore the bars and set them in their place,
    And as with bated breath and rapture pure
The sire looks upon his first-born's face,
    So he upon his Flag! What souls endure

In moments so supreme his soul endured!
    Nor even when he saw it in the dust,
To strife and blood and sorrow long inured,
    Did he forsake the dear and holy trust.
Smith gave the South her Flag. The best in him
    Was woven in its every sacred fold.
Though torn and tattered, faded, worn and dim,
    Our hearts enshrine it still in Memory's gold.

LELITA LEVER YOUNGE.
(Poet Laureate of Stonewall Jackson Chapter,
No. 1135, U. D. C., New Orleans, La.)

Major Smith's Own Story

When the Senators and Representatives of the seven Confederate States that had seceded February 1, 1861, met at Montgomery, Ala., the first business after organizing was to decide whether the new nation should have a new flag and new Constitution or fight under the "Stars and Stripes" and under the Constitution of the United States. The debate was short, both sides had strong arguments to offer. A new Constitution, composed of *native white citizens,* was adopted, and a committee was appointed to select a new flag. This committee advertised in the leading papers for designs of flags, to be sent to them at Montgomery. One of these went from Louisburg, N. C., where there was living a man, an original secessionist, who so hoped that the Confederacy would adopt a new flag and a new Constitution that he was ready with a design when the advertisement of "Flag Wanted" appeared. When this man, Orren Randolph Smith, was introduced by Gen. Julian S. Carr, commander-in-chief of the U. C. V. of North Carolina, at their reunion in Norfolk, September, 1910, he told the story of his flag in the following words:

"Three times have I been a soldier at my country's call, *twice* fighting under the Stars and Stripes and *once* under the 'Stars and Bars.' While with Taylor, south of the Rio Grande, a unit in that proud army that never let an enemy touch our flag; in Utah with Albert Sidney Johnston, 1857-1858, I learned what the flag meant to the men who were willing to give their lives for 'Old Glory' every day and every hour in the day. A soldier's flag must be his inspiration. It stands for home, kindred and country; it must be something more than a piece of bunting or the blending of bright colors.

"When at Sumter, that shot was fired that was heard around the world, I realized that a new country had been made and that the new nation must have a new flag, of the deepest, truest significance, to lead the 'Men in Gray' against the greatest odds and through the greatest difficulties that any soldiers have ever overcome since the world was made. The idea of my flag I took from the Trinity, 'Three in One.' The three bars were for the Church, State and.Press. Red represented State, legislative, judiciary and executive; white for Church, Father, Son and Holy Ghost; red for press, freedom of speech, freedom of conscience and liberty of press—all bound together by a field of blue (the heavens over all), bearing a Star for each State in the Confederation. The seven white stars, all the same size, were placed in a circle, showing that each State had equal rights and privileges irrespective of size or population. The circle, having neither head nor foot, stood for eternity, and signified 'You defend me and I'll protect you.' I had the flag all complete in my mind before the Confederate Congress advertised for models, and when the advertisement appeared I went to my friend, Miss Rebecca Murphy (she is now Mrs. W. B. Winborne, of Wilson, N. C.), and asked if she would make me a little flag, I'd tell her how. I tore the 'Bars and cut the Stars' and she sewed the stitches, and when finished the little flag was sent to Montgomery, with the suggestion that a star be added for each State that joined the Confederacy. The flag committee, as you all know, accepted the flag and named it 'The Stars and Bars.' They also adopted the suggestion, and it was not long before the flag bore eleven stars for the eleven Confederate States that voted for Jefferson Davis to be President. After the small flag was sent to Montgomery I bought dress goods from Barrow's store and asked Miss Rebecca to make me a large flag, 9x12 feet, for whether the flag committee accepted my model or not I was determined that one of my flags should be floating in the breeze. Splicing two tall saplings together, I made a pole one hundred feet high and planted it on the courthouse square at Louisburg, N. C. (where I was then living), and the flag was sent aloft on Monday, March 18, 1861, two months before North Carolina seceded. Over the flag was floating a long blue streamer, like an admiral has on his ship when 'homeward bound,' and on this pennant I had stars for each State that had seceded and one for North Carolina, for though my State was still in the Union I knew she was 'homeward bound.' This was the first Confederate flag ever raised in the Old North State, and this is how the 'Stars and Bars' came into existence, 'Dixie's Flag' that floated over the bravest and hardest to wear out soldiers ever encountered in any war."

Miss Murphy, who made the two flags, married first Dr. Germain Watson, and secondly W. B. Winborne. Her sister, Miss Sally Ann, refused to sew on the flag, saying she was "for the Union" and meant to marry a Yankee officer, and she did marry James A. Miller, lieutenant U. S. A. But while Mr. Smith and Miss Rebecca made the flags, Miss Sallie Ann played on the piano and sang Southern songs. In 1904 Mrs. Winborne was living at Pine Tops, N. C., and she appeared before W. L. Dunn, a justice of the peace (he was also postmaster), and made affidavit to the making of the Confederate model and the large flag that was displayed in Louisburg.

She is living today with her daughter, Mrs. H. T. Webb, on South Tarboro street, Wilson, N. C., and has become a member of the United Daughters of the Confederacy, for Mr. Smith said he wanted her to have a U. D. C. badge as it was "The Stars and Bars."

Honor to Designer of the Stars and Bars

In a long list of things for which the Confederacy stood pre-eminent, notably may stand the promptness with which due honor is meted out and the frequency with which the living hero feels the laurel on his brow. In such a category we would place the awarding of a gold medal by the North Carolina Division United Daughters of the Confederacy to Captain Orren Randolph Smith, who designed the flag of the Confederacy. The award was made a ceremony of the Lee-Jackson Day celebration in Henderson, Mr. Smith's present home, though it was at Louisburg the first flag was unfurled. The medal was presented first to the Orren Randolph Smith Chapter Children of the Confederacy (an enthusiastic body of 56 children named in his honor), who carried it to Major Smith, who has grown very infirm and was unable to attend the public meeting. The children recently served a lunch to the Henry L. Wyatt Camp, and with their leader, Mrs. Maurice J. O'Neil, are proving a most useful auxiliary to the Vance County Chapter.

The following is the speech made by Hon. W. H. Ruffin in presenting the medal:

"It is an unexpected pleasure to me to be called upon to present this medal or token of honor, for the designing of the original Stars and Bars; coming as I do, from Louisburg, it gives me an opportunity to state history upon this point, which, I regret to say, is now a disputed question. Of course, I am too young to state this history from my own observance, but I get this history from those who were living in Louisburg then and saw the Stars and Bars, first flung to the breeze, there in 1861, and from their statements and from that of Maj. Smith himself, I can point to the spot within three feet of where the flag pole stood. The second week in February, 1861, Major Smith called upon Miss Rebecca Murphy to make him a model of about a foot in length. The house in which she lived now stands in Louisburg and was, until its removal to a different site, a familiar landmark. Miss Murphy married a Mr. Winborne and now lives in Wilson, North Carolina, and her affidavit of these facts is now preserved. She also made the flag as raised by Maj. Smith. The raising of it, March 18, 1861, can even now be proven by Mr. Jordan Barrow, from whom the goods were purchased for the flag, Mr. Algernon S. Strother, Commander of McKinne Camp, U. C. V., and Mr. Eugene C. Cook, veterans and others, whom I might mention, though most of them are now passed to the Great Beyond. Maj. Smith stated to me that the three bars represented the Church, State and Press, and the power and freedom of each, that the seven stars represent the seven Confederate States, and above it was a long pennant, such as is put upon ships when homeward bound, and that it symbolized that Old North Carolina was likewise homeward bound into the Confederacy. There ought not to be any question that Maj. Orren Randolph Smith, then a resident of Franklin County, now a resident of your city, a veteran of three wars—Mexican, Utah and Confederate—designed and raised that flag first at Louisburg, in our State, and to him belongs the honor of giving to the Confederacy its emblem.

"Do not confuse this flag of the Confederacy with the battle flag afterwards adopted, for that battle flag is not in question. The United Daughters of the Confederacy of the State of North Carolina, pay this tribute to your distinguished townsman in recognition of his being the designer of the flag of the Great Confederacy, and commissions me to present to him in loving token of the honor due him for designing and raising the first Confederate flag, this beautiful medal or pendant which I hold in my hand; and it is with deepest regret that we note his absence on account of his feeble health, and pray that this old hero of three wars may be spared to us yet many years, and in his absence i take a profound pleasure in presenting the medal to the chapter of the Children of the Confederacy, which bears his name, with the request, that they carry it to him with the love and esteem of all Confederate organizations in the State."

Origin of the Stars and Bars

Paper prepared by Mrs. Fannie Ransom Williams, and read at the North Carolina Convention United Daughters of the Confederacy, in Tarboro, on Historical Evening, October 10, 1903.

Search back as far as we will along the pages of history, and we find that every tribe, every nation, has from time immemorial had some emblem or design, which was followed wherever it might lead, and for which men, aye, and women too, were willing to shed their blood if necessary.

Time passed and the earlier emblems of wood and skin gave place to those of handsomer material and finer design. Every nation upon this green earth has a flag peculiarly its own, a flag for which the noblest and best of its citizens, the man in the hut as well as the man in the palace, would sacrifice all save honor.

Again had years rolled by, and the clouds of war hung dark and heavy over our beloved Southland. History was in the making of a new nation, such history as had never before and will never again be written. A new nation was being born, and this new nation called for a new flag. The Confederate Congress, composed of representatives of the seven seceded states, sat in the halls of the Capitol at Montgomery, Ala. They had decided that the Confederate States of America must have a new flag of their own. Hence it was that they appointed a committee to select a design for this new flag.

As in most important matters, the newspapers are the means of communication with the people, so it was in this instance, and the Congressional Committee advertised for designs for the first national flag of the Confederacy, and it is to show to whom the honor of being the designer of this flag is due that this paper is written.

Orren Randolph Smith, born in that good old county of Warren, from whence have sprung so many noted sons, had served beneath the Stars and Stripes in the war with Mexico, and again against the movement in Utah, under Albert Sidney Johnston. He was loyal and true to his country, but he was a true son of the South, and above all was a proud North Carolinian. He was a firm believer in "states' rights," and also in secession. With no lack of insight into matters, Mr. Smith saw what was coming, and realized the need of a new flag. Hence it was that when the call for designs appeared Mr. Smith had already pictured in his mind's eye the flag he wanted to see.

In his own handwriting he has left us a statement of how he conceived that flag, saying:

"It was designed upon the idea of the Trinity—hence the three bars—Church, State and Press. The Church stood for Father, Son and Holy Ghost; the State for legislative, judicial and executive; the Press for free speech, liberty of conscience and the right to be heard. The colors stood, white for purity; blue for constancy; red for defiance. Each State in the Confederacy, at the time of the design, was represented by a star, and there were only seven upon the original that was made and flown to the breeze on the corner of the courthouse square in Louisburg, Franklin County, N. C., 1861. It was made by Miss Catherine Rebecca Murphy, assisted by her aunt, Miss Nora Sykes. The material was bought of Jordan Barrow, and was good dress stuff, that floated light in the breeze. The original flag was nine by twelve feet. The model sent to the Congress in Montgomery, Ala., was about twelve by nine inches, but the large flag was an exact reproduction. There were only seven states in the Confederate Congress on its assembling, only seven states had up to that time seceded, and they advertised for designs. I was ready with mine before the advertisement appeared as I was an original secessionist."

Such is Major Smith's own account of the designing and making of the flag. Now for one moment we will see what the lady has to say on the subject. But before proceeding, perhaps a word of explanation may prevent confusion. Miss Rebecca Murphy was at that time Mrs. Watson, a widow, and she later married a second time, so she is now Mrs. C. R. Winborne, hence the different names, all referring to the same party used in our affidavits. Mrs. Winborne says:

"When the War between the States began I was living at my old home, Louisburg, N. C. As I have been asked to tell all I know about the making of the Confederate flag, known as the Stars and Bars, I consider it both a duty and privilege to make this affidavit, so that in the days to come there may be no doubt as to the identity of the man who designed the first flag of the Confederacy.

"Early in 1861, the second week in February, my old friend, Orren Randolph Smith, brought me some material and asked me to make him a flag, and that he would tell me exactly how to do it; for the Confederacy had decided that a new flag was to be used in the war for states' rights, and a committee had been appointed to decide upon a model and they had advertised for models, and he, Mr. Smith, wanted to have this little flag of his own design to send as a model.

The design that I copied was composed of a blue field and three stripes; one white between two red, and on the blue field, which extended across the end of the white and one red stripe, I sewed seven white stars in a circle, a star for each state that had seceded.

This small flag was about a foot long. The design was made by Orren Randolph Smith, in Louisburg, N. C., and the flag was packed and sent to Montgomery, Ala., and was later the design, without alterations, that was accepted by the committee as the world now knows."

Thus we have a very clear statement of the subject from both designer and maker of this model, and they agree in every particular, in date, design and material. Both continue in their affidavits to tell of the making and raising of a large copy of this model on March 18, 1861.

John H. Williamson, of Louisburg, says under oath that he "remembers distinctly when Miss Rebecca Watson made the first Confederate flag, although he does not remember who designed it," thus corroborating Mrs. Winborne's statement.

Rev. Charles D. Malone, in a letter dated July 2, 1913, says:

"I am perfectly satisfied your father raised the flag in Louisburg on March 18, 1861, and it was understood by everybody that she (Miss Murphy) helped your father make the flag. Col. Yarborough and Mr. A. S. Strothers will corroborate all I say. That they know it to be true as to the fact of your father (Major Smith) being the one that designed and raised the flag, and that Miss Rebecca Murphy did the sewing. There is no doubt in the minds of any that the general opinion prevailed that Major Smith designed the flag and that Mrs. Winborne made both the model and the large flag raised in Louisburg on March 18, 1861."

Besides these we have a number of other affidavits that Major Smith designed the flag.

Major Smith and Mrs. Winborne have both plainly described the design of the first flag as the model was sent to Montgomery the middle of February, 1861. Now the "Committee on a Proper Flag for the Confederate States of America," appointed by Congress, in its report of March 4, 1861, is as follows:

"That the flag of of the Confederate States of America shall consist of a red field with a white space extending horizontally through the center, and equal in width to one-third the width of the flag. The red spaces above and below to be of the same width as the white. The union blue extending down through the white space and stopping at the lower red space. In the center of the union a circle of white stars, corresponding in number with the states of the Confederacy."

Such is the proof that North Carolina holds that one of her sons really designed the Stars and Bars. There was no necessity for the Congressional committee to make a single change in the design sent by Major Smith. We find the design described in the adoption of the flag by Congress and the one by Major Smith *exactly* the same in every particular.

We do not deny the fact that there was another design sent. In fact the contestant for this honor with Mr. Smith sent *three,* somewhat similar, we acknowledge, but not one of the exact design, as we will show if you will bear with us for a few moments longer.

Mr. Nicola Marschall, in a statement given to a Louisville correspondent of the Montgomery (Alabama) *Advertiser* on June 11, 1911, states that some time the latter part of April or May, "the designs were painted by him." In Mr. P. D. Harrison's book on flags Mr. Marschall says "some time in the late spring." Hence you see Mr. Marschall is by no means certain of his dates, and even places them after the adoption of the design March 4, 1861.

In the same newspaper is printed a copy of the three designs, "dashed off on a card" by Mr. Marschall. In the first and second designs we find the white stripe is double the width of the red ones. In the first the blue union with the white stars is at the left end of the white stripe; in the second we find this union placed in the middle of the white stripe. In the third design, the white and red stripes are the same width, but the blue union extends across one red and half the white stripe. Compare this last design with that of Major Smith's and you will find in the former we have the union extending only across half the white stripe, while in Major Smith's and in the Stars and Bars as adopted it extends entirely across the white, and why should the Congressional committee change one man's design when, another man's exactly what they wanted, was in their hands?

When the unprejudiced reader has examined the designs of both the claimants and the affidavits appended to this paper, the honor of being the designer will unhesitatingly be accorded, where we have proven it to belong, to Orren Randolph Smith, of North Carolina.

The Stars and Bars---Who Designed It?

Paper prepared for the Contemporary Club, Henderson, N. C., by Hon. T. M. Pitt-man, LL. D., member of the North Carolina Historical Commission.

The Confederate States of America had four flags. That known as the Stars and Bars was the first adopted. Its design was reported to the Provisional Congress on March 4, 1861, just one month after the formation of the Southern Confederacy. The committee, of which William Porcher Miles, of South Carolina, was chairman, received designs from all over the South. One hundred and twenty-nine of these, with the letters accompanying them, were pasted in an old volume of treasury blanks and filed away with the captured Confederate archives in the War Department at Washington. They are probably still there, but seem not to have been accessible to those seeking information upon the subject of this paper.

The general features of this flag were so similar to the Stars and Stripes as to create confusion in battle, both sides being misled by the resemblance. This likeness was potent at the time of its adoption and contributed to its selection in deference to a sentiment of deep attachment to the old flag. Frank Carpenter, writing in *Lippincott's Magazine,* April, 1885, says:

"From the designs and letters it can be seen how general was the desire throughout the South to retain all that was possible of the old flag. The greater part of the designs are made up of modifications of the stars and stripes in all conceivable shapes, and there is scarcely a writer who does not wish that the associations of the old flag may be preserved in the new. One letter recommends a design because it retains all the hallowed associations which have for years clustered around the 'stars and stripes' of a nation once the most glorious the world ever beheld, and of which nation the Southern States were but lately its proudest element, blest in its privileges, blest in its widespread fraternal love, and equal in the possession of all its common glories, past, present, and prospective. * * * This feeling for the stars and stripes was indeed so strong that the convention dared not neglect it." To the same effect is Harrison's "The Stars and Stripes and Other American Flags." P. 325, *Ib.*

Unfortunately the committee failed to name the author of the design, and rival claimants now contend for that distinction. The situation, however, is measurably relieved by the fact that the contention is confined to two persons, viz., Orren Randolph Smith, late of Henderson, North Carolina, and Nicola Marschall, of Louisville, Kentucky.

The claim of Major Smith became the subject of newspaper discussion during the later years of the last century, and was undisputed until February, 1904, when Mr. Marschall asserted his right, through the *Lost Cause,* a periodical published in Louisville. So far neither of these gentlemen or their friends have been able to produce any official record or contemporaneons writing in support of their respective contentions, and we are left to the statements of the parties themselves and such collateral support as may be derived from other sources. It is the purpose of this paper to state the known facts as fully as possibly and deduce from them the conclusions which shall seem most probably correct under all the circumstances.

Mr. Marschall is an artist, who was born in Prussia in 1829 and came to America in 1849. He located at Marion, Alabama, where he formed pleasant associations and acquired reputation and popularity as a painter of portraits. The statement of his claim in the *Lost Cause* is as follows:

"Texas had first seceded on February 1, 1861. No flag had been adopted, and calls were made for a suitable design. Mrs. Lockett, being a friend of the young artist, who by this time had distinguished himself in his art, went to him and told him the Confederate Government wanted a flag, and suggested he should design one similar to the United States flag. He took his pencils and made two designs. The one red and white with the blue field in the upper left corner and seven stars, the number of States that had at that time seceded."

In response to Mr. Harrison's inquiry for further particulars, he wrote, December 16, 1904, "I have nothing to add to the article in the *Lost Cause,* as that states all I know and

Flag of the Confederacy and the Two Designs That Were Rejected.—From the
Marschall flag article in the Montgomery Advertiser.

the dates I have forgotten." Mr. Harrison then upon Mr. Marschall's reference wrote to three different people for information relating to his design, "but neither one has any personal knowledge of it."

The foregoing information concerning Mr. Marschall is taken from "The Stars and Stripes," etc. pages 331-334.

In the *Montgomery Advertiser* of June 11, 1911, is an apparently authoritative article giving a circumstantial account of his designing the flag. It is not substantially different from the *Lost Cause* statement, except that the date of his design is given as "towards the latter part of April or early in May, several weeks after the opening of hostilities," and a cut of his design is printed which differs from that actually adopted and used in that the blue field in the upper left hand corner does not extend down through the upper red bar and the white bar, but only half way the white—*i. e.,* only one-half the depth of the flag instead of two-thirds. This statement says that he made three instead of two designs.

He only learned from Mrs. Lockett "a month or so later" that his drawing was accepted. "Later I saw the flag at the head of a body of soldiers attired in gray uniforms"; this last a rather uncomfortably guarded statement.

This is apparently the only information bearing upon Mr. Marschall's claim.

Major Smith was born in Warren County, North Carolina, December 18, 1827. His grandfather, Samuel Smith, was a soldier of the Revolution, who lived to the age of ninety-six years and was blind a long time before his death. Orren was the companion and guide of this old man, and his audience of one, into whose willing ears were poured the stories of military achievement and the civil struggles for popular liberty. The youth was of a highly imaginative and excitable temperament which was manifest throughout his long life. While yet a youth he discarded his school books and enlisted in Company H, First North Carolina Regiment, for service in the Mexican War. After his return from Mexico he enlisted under Colonel Albert Sidney Johnston for service against the Mormons.

At the breaking out of the Civil War, Major Smith was back

in North Carolina an ardent secessionist and intensly impatient of the Union spirit then dominant in that State.

While he was chafing under these conditions the Confederacy was formed at Montgomery, Alabama. Its call for the submission of designs for a National flag came to him as one held in leash and offered at least one opportunity for coming in touch with the forward movement of the South. His restless spirit had anticipated the demand and his fancy had already wrought out the design since known as the Stars and Bars, which recognized the common demand for a flag having kinship with the *old* flag, and was to him also emblematic in its colors, etc., of various things which he thought significant of the new national impulse. He engaged the assistance of Mrs. Rebecca Watson, a young widow living at Louisburg, N. C., who made for him a model flag about 12 by 15 inches in size, which was forwarded to Montgomery and, as he was later informed through the newspapers, was accepted. Immediately after he learned of the adoption of his design Major Smith procured goods from the store of Mr. J. S. Barrow, at Louisburg, and again sought the assistance of Mrs. Watson in the making of a large flag after the same design, 9 by 12 feet in size. This was completed on March 17, and raised near the courthouse in Louisburg on March 18, 1861.

The various details of the foregoing statement are supported by affidavits of credible witnesses who have personal knowledge of the facts.

Mrs. Watson (now Mrs. Winborne), says "Early in 1861, the second week in February, my old friend Orren Randolph Smith, brought me some material and asked me to make him a flag, he would tell me how to do it, for the Confederacy had decided that a new flag was to be used * * * and he * * * was going to send in this little flag as a model."

"The design was composed of a blue field and three stripes one white and two red, and on the blue field I sewed seven white stars in a circle, a star for each State that up to that time had seceded.

"This small flag was about a foot long. This design was made by Orren Randolph Smith, in Louisburg, North Carolina, and the flag was made by me under his directions, packed and sent to Montgomery, Alabama and was accepted."

Mrs. Watson gives the details of making and raising the large flag, noting the refusal of her sister to assist in the making because of her Union sentiment, etc.

Mrs. Sue Jasper Sugg, Tarboro, N. C., tells of being in Louisburg at the home of Mrs. Watson and of the making of the model and the large flag under Major Smith's directions, which were "exactly like the flag now called the Stars and Bars, and that she was present and saw Mr. Smith when he raised the large flag."

John H. Williamson "remembers distinctly when Mrs. Rebecca Watson made the first Confederate flag, but is unable to say who designed it." Its raising "was superintended by Mr. O. R. Smith."

Algernon S. Strother tells how Orren R. Smith in March, 1861, designed and raised a Confederate States flag in the northwest corner of the courthouse square in Louisburg. I remember distinctly how it looked; that it was made of good purchased of Mr. J. S. Barrow, who had a general merchandise store, and was made by Miss Becky Murphy (the maiden name of Mrs. Watson). "The flag had three stripes of red and white and stars in the corner, and it hung where Mr. Smith placed (it) until I went off to the war in Company K, Thirty-second Regiment, Franklin Rifles."

These affidavits may be seen complete in the appendix hereto.

Jos. John Allen, a half-brother of Major Smith, gives in the Raleigh *News and Observer,* of October 19, 1913, the following interesting account of their mother's uneasiness over Orren's rashness and of his own visit to the flag, etc.

As I am a half brother of the late Orren Randolph Smith, I have heretofore deemed it officious and unbecoming to say much along this line, but in the interest of truth and of history I shall now tell just what I know about this flag and what I shall say is the truth and nothing but the truth:

I was, at the time of the raising of this flag, a barefooted boy of fourteen years of age, and it was on one Monday afternoon, March 18th, 1861, that I had returned from a field where I had been to see some work being done by my father's negroes, and I found our mother in a fit of nervous excitement over "Orren's hasty adventure at secession," and by her I was informed that he had gone over to town to raise "The Liberty Pole," a term used by our ancestors during the Revolution, and she not knowing what to call the secession flag.

As I had this news broken to me so suddenly, I was impatient for the next morning to come, that I might go over to Louisburg and see what that secession monstrosity meant, and finishing my breakfast I put out afoot and soon found myself under its moving folds where it had been erected near where Hicks' corner now is on Main street in Louisburg.

The pole, made in sections of two poplars, was cut on my father's land and by Bill Allen, colored, a slave of my father, and who was then in the employ of Orren Smith, and who is still living and will testify to the part he took in cutting the pole and its erection.

Among the school boys still living who will testify to the Stars and Bars on this date and its erection are the following: Rev. Charles D. Malone, of Washington, N. C.; Dr. Wm. C. Person, Orlando, Fla.; Hugh D. Egerton, Charles Harris, W. W. Green, Frank Ballard, Dr. R. E. King, of Louisburg, N. C.

The soldiers who volunteered under this flag in the first company of the county, "Franklin Rifles," under the late William Furnifold Green, are: Dixon G. Conn, Raleigh, N. C.; Hon. Thomas S. Collie, Castalia, N. C.; Col. W. H. Yarborough, Louisburg, N. C.; Josiah A. May, and several others who will testify that the Stars and Bars were first seen and heard of in the good old town of Louisburg, N. C. Now, to those who claim any Stars and Bars that antedate this I shall say, "Let it come and let the truth prevail."

Trusting that this statement may meet the eyes of the North Carolina Daughters,

I am, most respectfully,

JOSEPH JOHN ALLEN.

Louisburg, October 14, 1913.

From this available information it seems reasonable to infer:

1. That Mr. Marschall's work was so casual as to make no decided impression upon his mind either before or after his work was done. There is no model or flag from his design subject to comparison with flags in actual service.

2. That his design furnished to and published in The Montgomery *Advertiser* is unlike the flag actually adopted and used, a difference that is material in view of the great similarity of many of the designs.

3. That Major Smith's work was not causal but marked by great enthusiasm, earnestness and deep concern, calculated to make a lasting impression upon his own mind, and on others. His flag was raised and kept flying for months, at least, in one of the most intelligent communities in the South, subject to criticism and comparison with flags in actual service. He is corroborated in every material detail by the affidavits of credible witnesses.

Major Smith's claim appears to be unquestionably sustained by the greater weight of the evidence and ought to be admitted.

Henderson, N. C., October 28, 1913.

Affidavits

Mrs. Catherine Rebecca Winborne

North Carolina—Wilson County.

When the War Between the States began I was living at my old home, Louisburg, N. C., the widow of Mr. German Watson. And since I have been asked to tell all I know of the designing and making of the Confederate flag, known as the Stars and Bars, I consider it both a duty and privilege to make this affidavit, so that in the days to come there may be no doubt as to the identity of the man who designed the Stars and Bars, the first flag of the Confederate States of America.

Early in 1861, the second week in February, my old friend, Orren Randolph Smith, brought me some material and asked me to make him a flag, and that he would tell me exactly how to do it, for the Confederacy had decided that a new flag was to be used in the War for States' Rights, and a committee had been appointed to decide upon a model, and this committee had advertised for models and he, Mr. Smith, wanted to have this little flag of his own design to send as a model.

The design that I copied was composed of a blue field and three stripes, one white between two red, and on the blue field, which extended across the end of the white and one red stripe, I sewed seven white stars in a circle, a star for each State that up to that time had seceded.

This small flag was about a foot long. The design was made by Orren Randolph Smith, in Louisburg, N. C., and the flag was made by me under his direction and when finished was packed and sent to Montgomery, Ala., and was later the design, without any alterations, that was accepted by the committee, as all the world now knows, and everywhere it is honored and treated with reverence.

As soon as Mr. Smith learned that his design was accepted as "the flag of the Confederate States of America," the day following he again came to me and brought material to make a large flag in accordance with his model, and with my assistance a large flag, identical in every particular with the small model, sent to Montgomery was made. We enjoyed our work, talking and laughing as old friends do when together and interested in their work, and then, we had no idea of the terrific struggle that was coming, nor of the fierce fighting that was to be done under and for that flag.

My sister, Sarah Ann, would not help us to make either flag; said she was "for the Union," and intended to marry a Yankee officer (and she did), so while we worked on the flags she played and sang different Southern songs.

We sewed and worked on the large flag as hard as we could, but did not get it finished by Saturday night, so we completed it on Sunday, March 17, 1861, and early Monday morning Mr. Smith raised this flag in Louisburg, N. C., it being the first Confederate flag ever displayed in North Carolina, and two months before the Old North State left the Union.

Over the flag Mr. Smith had floating in the breeze, a long blue pennant, like an admiral's pennant on his ship when homeward bound, and on this pennant were nine white stars. He said that though North Carolina was still in the Union she was homeward bound, and this was the first significant straw that showed which way the wind was blowing.

CATHERINE REBECCA (her X mark) WINBORNE.

Witness as to mark:

GEO. STRONACH.

Sworn to before me this 30th day of June, 1913.

GEO. STRONACH, *Notary Public.*

Mrs. Sue Jasper Sugg

TARBORO, N. C.

Having been in Louisburg, in February, 1861, and being a friend of both Mrs. Rebecca Watson and Mr. Orren Randolph Smith, I was in Mrs. Watson's house while she was sewing on the Confederate flag model to be sent to the Confederate Congress. I know she was making it for that purpose, know that Orren Smith designed it, and heard him tell her how to make it; and I also know that model was sent to the Flag Committee in Montgomery, and we all know it was Mr. Smith's design when accepted. The model was exactly like the flag now called the Stars and Bars.

I also knew and saw Mrs. Watson when she was making the "large flag" which was raised on the courthouse square in the town of Louisburg, N. C., on March 18, 1861. This large flag was exactly like the small one sent to Montgomery by Mr. Smith. I was present and saw Mr. Smith when he raised it.   (Signed) MRS. SUE JASPER SUGG.

North Carolina—Edgecombe County.

Personally appeared before me this day, Mrs. Sue Jasper Sugg, who being first duly sworn, says that the facts above stated are true to the best of her knowledge and belief.

This October 10, 1913.   (Signed) A. T. WALSTON.

(Legal Seal)   Clerk Superior Court.

C. C. Harris

North Carolina—Franklin County.

C. C. Harris, being duly sworn according to law, says: That he remembers well the year when the soldiers went to the front and that early in the said year, 1861, he was in Louisburg when Orren Smith raised a flag at the courthouse square; he was present and saw the flag when it was brought to be drawn up on the pole, and by some means it became entangled in the rope and Mr. Smith climbed the pole with the aid of the rope and disentangled the flag, and it was then drawn to the top of the pole; there were a good many people in town that day, and affiant distinctly remembers that as the flag floated out on the breeze Mr. William F. Green, afterwards a Colonel in the Confederate Army, took off his hat and waived it over his head and said "May God give it victory."

(Signed) C. C. HARRIS.

Sworn to and subscribed before me this September 6, 1913.

THOS. B. WILSON.

Algernon S. Strother

North Carolina—Franklin County.

I, Algernon S. Strother, a native of Louisburg, Franklin County, North Carolina, being first duly sworn, do depose and say:

That in the month of March, 1861, Orren R. Smith, who was then in Louisburg, North Carolina, designed and raised a Confederate States flag on the northwest corner of the courthouse square, in Louisburg. I recall distinctly how it looked; that it was made of goods purchased of Mr. J. S. Barrow, who had a general merchandise store in Louisburg; that it was made by Miss Becky Murphy, who also lived in Louisburg, near where the Seaboard Air Line Railway depot stands today; that Mr. Smith had one Bill Allen, a colored man, to get him a pole to raise the flag on, and the pole he brought was too short, and Bill was sent for another one, and he spliced the poles, making one tall pole. This flag had three stripes of red and white, and stars in the corner, and it hung where Mr. Smith placed it until I went off to the war in Company K, Thirty-second Regiment, Franklin Rifles.

I have been told that it hung there till the troops in Sherman's army came .by and cut it down, though, being in the Confederate Army and away from Louisburg then, I have no personal knowledge of how or when it was taken down.

(Signed) ALGERNON S. STROTHER.

Sworn to and subscribed before me this 5th day of September, 1913.   J. J. BARROW,

Clerk Superior Court of Franklin County.

Friends, Contributors and Helpers

Last year when the North Carolina Division, United Daughters of the Confederacy held their convention at Salisbury, Mrs. T. W. Thrash, Recording Secretary of the division, on behalf of Major Smith, presented to the Daughters a beautiful flag which was accepted with thanks, but the State Historian asked for proofs.

One of the first important acts of Miss Carrie Leazar as Historian of the North Carolina Division was to ask Mrs. Fannie Ransom Williams to write a paper on "The Stars and Bars." This year, on Historical Evening, at Tarboro, the claims of Major Smith were clearly proven and affidavits read and accepted by the Division, with hearty applause.

After Mrs. Williams had so acceptably presented his flag to the United Daughters of the Confederacy, at Washington, Major Smith asked her, as the daughter of his friend and kinsman, General Robert Ransom, to write for him, the story of his flag.

The original affidavits given here with those of Rev. C. D. Malone, Messrs. J. A. May, Hugh Edgerton, Wm. J. King, J. H. Williams and William S. Allen; and the exact copies of the three models painted by Mr. Nicola Marschall, and the model made under the direction of Major Smith, have been filed in the United Daughters of the Confederacy Archives, at Raleigh, N. C., by the efficient Historian, Miss Leazar.

For hearty coöperation and assistance in collecting the history of "The Stars and Bars," besides those whose names have been mentioned, special thanks are due, and are hereby gratefully given to the following:

Mr. P. D. Harrison, author of "The Stars and Stripes and other American Flags," Manchester, N. H.

Gen. Julian S. Carr, Commander-in-Chief N. C. Div. U. C., V., Durham, N. C.

Colonel S. A. Cunningham editor of the *Confederate Veteran,* Nashville, Tenn.

Col. T. C. DeLeon, author of the "Belles Beaux and Brains of the Sixties," Mobile, Ala.

Colonel F. A. Olds, Dean of the City Press, Raleigh, N. C.

Mr. M. O. Sherrill, State Librarian, Raleigh, N. C.

Mrs. N. V. Randolph, President Richmond Chapter, U. D. C., Richmond, Va.

Miss Rebecca Cameron, Honorary Historian, North Carolina Division, U. D. C., Hillsboro, N. C.

Mrs. J. P. Winston, President J. J. Davis Chapter, U. D. C., Louisburg, N. C.

Mrs. R. H. Davis, Registrar State Division, U. D. C., Louisburg, N. C.

Mr. A. F. Johnson, Editor of the *Franklin Times,* Louisburg, N. C.

Mrs. Doane Herring, former President, and Mrs. F. A. Woodard, President of the John W. Dunton Chapter, U. D. C., Wilson, N. C.

Mrs. Joseph R. Estes, Birmingham, Ala.

Newspapers of Washington, D. C., Maryland, Virginia, North Carolina, South Carolina, Georgia, Alabama, Mississippi, Kentucky and others.